Sonia Mehta is a children's writer who believes that sparking off a child's imagination opens up a world of adventure. She has been writing for children for over two decades. Her body of work is wide-ranging—she created one of India's first dedicated children's newspaper sections; conceptualized the *Cadbury Bournvita Quiz Contest* for TV; and has written books, songs, poems and stories for leading publishers in India, several African nations, the USA and the UK.

She lives in Mumbai and runs Quadrum Solutions, a content company she co-founded. She is also the co-founder of PodSquad, a retail children's edutainment brand that firmly believes that children learn best when they are having fun.

Most days, Sonia can be found pounding away at her computer—when she is not playing with her dachshunds, the two little loves of her life.

Read More in the Junior Lives Series

Mother Teresa

Junior Lives

Mahatma Gandhi

Sonia Mehta

Illustrated by Aditya Krishnamurthy

PUFFIN BOOKS
An imprint of Penguin Random House

PUFFIN BOOKS

USA | Canada | UK | Ireland | Australia
New Zealand | India | South Africa | China

Puffin Books is part of the Penguin Random House group of companies whose addresses can be found at global.penguinrandomhouse.com

Published by Penguin Random House India Pvt. Ltd
7th Floor, Infinity Tower C, DLF Cyber City,
Gurgaon 122 002, Haryana, India

Penguin
Random House
India

First published in Puffin Books by Penguin Random House India 2017

Text and illustrations copyright © Quadrum Solutions Pvt. Ltd 2017
Series copyright © Penguin Random House India 2017

All rights reserved

10 9 8 7 6 5 4 3 2 1

The views and opinions expressed in this book are the author's own and the facts are as reported by her, which have been verified to the extent possible, and the publishers are not in any way liable for the same.

The information in this book is based on research from bona fide sites and published books and is true to the best of the author's knowledge at the time of going to print. Conversations have been created to enliven and narrate the story and are not verbatim utterances. The author is not liable for any further changes or development in incidents occurring post the publication of this book.

ISBN 9780143428268

Design and layout by Quadrum Solutions Pvt. Ltd
Printed at Replika Press Pvt. Ltd, India

This book is sold subject to the condition that it shall not, by way of trade or otherwise, be lent, resold, hired out, or otherwise circulated without the publisher's prior consent in any form of binding or cover other than that in which it is published and without a similar condition including this condition being imposed on the subsequent purchaser.

www.penguin.co.in

Contents

1. Childhood Days 1
2. London Calling 14
3. Off to Africa 25
4. Fighting Injustice 32
5. Soldiers of Truth 39
6. Coming Home to India 52
7. We Will Not Cooperate 59
8. The Final Fight 71
9. Gandhi Factopedia 81
10. Timeline 88
11. Bibliography 90

1 Childhood Days

The thirteen-year-old lad was impatient.
He wanted to get back to his friends, who were having a great time playing outdoors. But here he was—stuck indoors, made to dress up in clothes that were icky and uncomfortable.

'Can I go now?' he asked his mother, trying to shrug off the elaborate outfit she was trying to get him to wear.

'No, Mohan,' she replied. 'You can't go play with your friends today. It's your wedding day.'

That young boy was Mohandas Karamchand Gandhi. At thirteen years of age, he was about to get married to a girl who was just a little older than he was. His family would never have believed it then, but this boy was to grow up to become one of the world's greatest leaders, who would lead India to freedom. He showed people a non-violent way of life. Millions of people adored him and gave him titles like **Father of the Nation, Bapu** (meaning father) and **Mahatma** (meaning great soul). What an incredible achievement for such an ordinary boy, born to such ordinary parents!

A Happy Family

Young Mohan (for that was what his family called him) was born to Karamchand and Putlibai on 2 October 1869. Theirs was a large, happy family. Mohan had a sister and two brothers—all older than him, so you can imagine how much he was loved and petted. The family was quite wealthy and lived in a big, three-storeyed house in the Indian port-city of Porbandar, in what is now Gujarat. Karamchand was an educated man. The ruler of Rajkot admired him and made him the diwan of Porbandar. As diwan, he managed the business of the state. People respected Karamchand a lot and came to him for advice.

> **Did You Know?**
> As a little boy, Mohan was so timid that he was scared of ghosts, thieves and snakes. He was even afraid of the dark.

When Mohan was a young boy, he was very shy. He would spend all his time with his books. This made him very thoughtful. However, he didn't love studies; in fact, he found maths rather hard. But he was a good student overall, and his teachers thought well of him.

One day, Mohan got his father's permission to see a play about a king named Raja Harishchandra. The special thing about this king was that he never lied, no matter what happened to him. Mohan was so impressed by this play that he swore to never tell a lie in his life.

Always, Always Truthful

One morning, Mohan's class was given a spelling test. Mohan knew all the spellings, except that of 'kettle'. The English teacher, keen to prove that he was a good teacher, wanted all his students to know every spelling so that he could impress his superiors. When he saw that Mohan was unsure, he prodded him to peep at his neighbour's slate and see the spelling.

'But that would be cheating,' an aghast Mohan thought. He refused to look at his neighbour's slate, and eventually was the only boy in class who did not get all his spellings right. But that didn't bother him. He was more bothered that his teacher had told him to cheat.

This is how one of Mohan's report cards read:

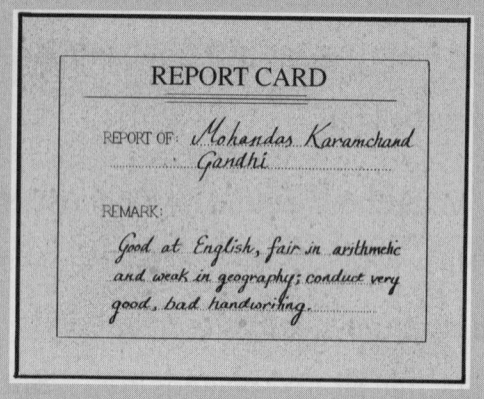

> **REPORT CARD**
>
> REPORT OF: Mohandas Karamchand Gandhi
>
> REMARK:
> Good at English, fair in arithmetic and weak in geography; conduct very good, bad handwriting.

Mohan hated the fact that his handwriting was so terrible. He felt really bad about this all his life.

One of the only times Mohan lied was when he was in his early teens. He stole some gold from his brother and sold it. But it wasn't for himself. He gave the money to his other brother to help him get out of debt. He couldn't sleep that night. He tossed and turned, feeling awful. Finally, he confessed to his father. He was ready for any punishment. But instead of getting upset, Mohan's father wept. He was hurt that his son had lied, but happy he had confessed.

Playing Married

Mohan was in Standard Three when he got married to Kasturba. The year was 1883. In those days, children got married very young in India and to whoever their parents chose for them. Mohan's parents chose Kasturba—a simple, happy but strong-minded girl from Porbandar.

In the beginning, marriage for Mohan and Kasturba was like a game. They were playmates. But as time went on, Mohan began to bully Kasturba. He began to control her. He wanted to know where she went, what she wore, whom she met.

> **Oh Really?**
> Mohan had to lose a whole year of school because he got married. Imagine that!

'Where are you going?' he would ask her when he saw her getting dressed to go out.

'To the temple, with my friends,' she would answer, tossing her plait over her shoulder defiantly.

'You can't go. I won't allow you to,' Mohan would say obstinately. But Kasturba was no meek miss. She refused to be bullied by her young husband. They would sulk and not talk to each other for days—just like young children do. Mohan was simply following what he saw around him.

As he grew up, not only did he realize that what he had done in those early days was wrong, but he wrote about how child marriage itself was not a good idea. Not only were children too young to understand the responsibilities that came with marriage, their education took a hit as well. Women did not have the opportunities to get an education. He tried his best to change such habits and beliefs in people.

Did You Know?

Just three years after they got married, Kasturba had a baby. She was seventeen, Mohan was sixteen. But the baby did not survive. This convinced Mohan even more in later life that getting married so early is not a good idea at all!

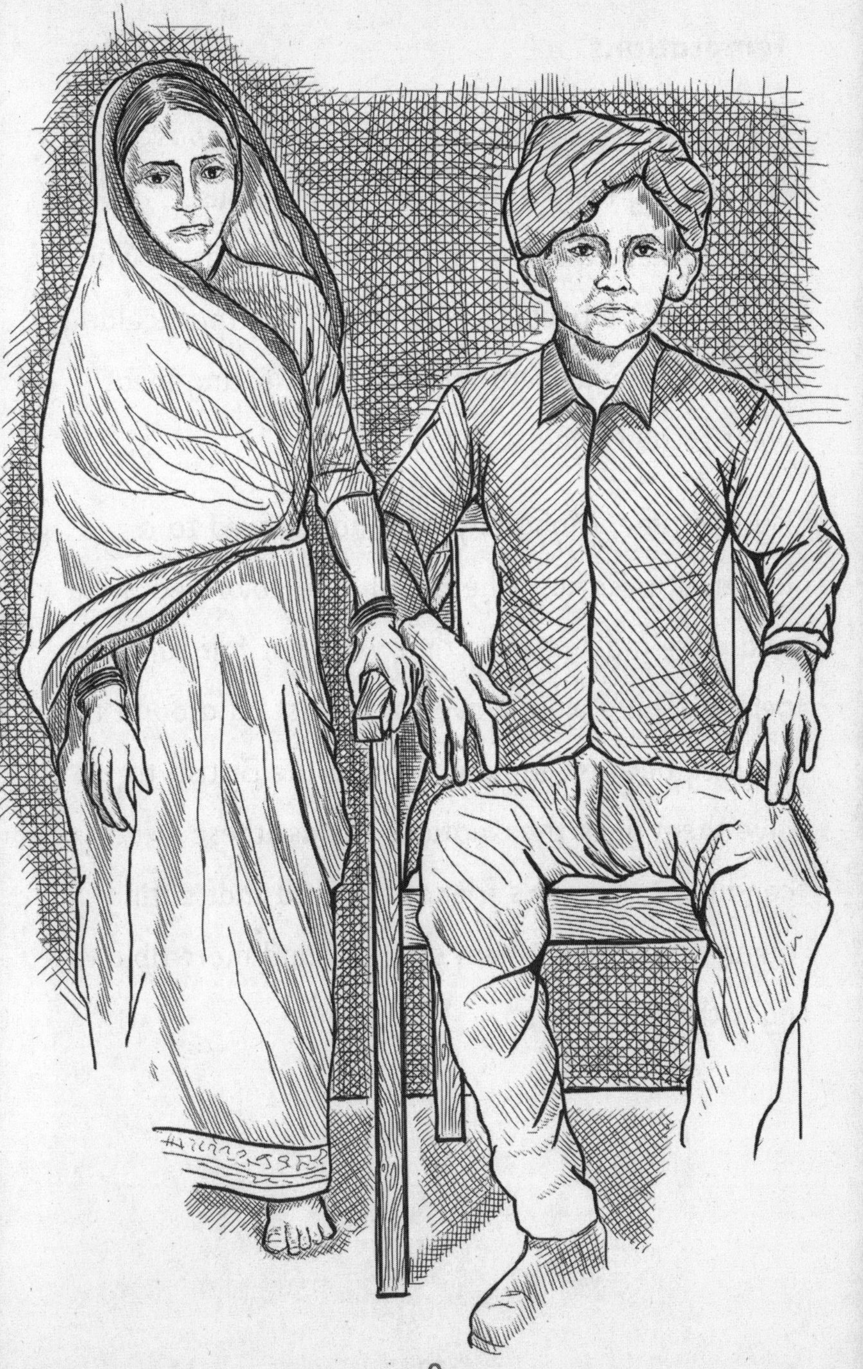

Temptations

Just like it happens to all of us, Mohan was tempted by his friends to be adventurous. One of these adventures was to eat meat. It was an adventure because Mohan's family (particularly his mother) was very religious, and eating meat went totally against their religion.

By this time, Mohan's family had moved to a larger city, Rajkot. The British had colonized India and were making rules that were not fair to Indian people. There were waves of protest all around the country because Indians wanted the British to give them back their nation. Amidst these conditions, Mohan's friends believed that eating meat would make them stronger and more able to fight the British.

THE RULE OF THE BRITISH

The British, who were always looking to expand their empire, had colonized India. This means that they had taken full control over running India. They set up a trading company called the East India Company. But this was more than a trading company. It had its own troops. It made political decisions. The first war for independence, also called the Sepoy Mutiny, was fought in 1857. There was so much bloodshed that the East India Company was abolished. India came directly under British rule. The British made many laws that were unfair to Indians. Indians could not hold certain posts; they could not visit certain places; they could not vote. Naturally, this angered Indians. They began to revolt. This led to a long fight against the British. When Mohan grew up, this was the fight he led. Finally, in 1947, the British left and India became independent.

'See how big and strong the British people are,' his friends told Mohan. 'That is because they eat meat and we eat only vegetables.' Mohan was convinced. He thought his friends were right, that he would actually get stronger if he ate meat. So he started eating it, even though he knew that if his mother, Putlibai, ever found out, she would be devastated.

Mohan himself found it very hard. The first time he ate mutton, he had nightmares. 'I felt that a live goat was crying inside me,' he wrote many years later. He never really grew to like meat, and soon gave it up when he found that it was of no help in getting the British to go away.

Losing His Father

As a teenager, Mohan was devoted to his parents. He would rush home after school to look after his father, who was bedridden. He would massage his feet and spend time with him. Sadly for Mohan, he was not by his father's bedside when he died. But his father had a deep influence on young Mohan. People of all faiths visited him—Christians, Muslims and Jains. Thanks to him, Mohan believed that people of all religions must live together peacefully.

2 London Calling

The year was 1887. Mohan had finished school. He started college but didn't find it interesting at all. After his father's death, Mohan's older brother Laxmidas began relying on old family friends for advice on running the household. One such friend suggested that Mohan be sent to London to study law. His family was confused. No one from their family had ever been abroad— let alone at such a young age.

'He will be led astray,' Putlibai lamented. She thought he would end up getting bad habits like eating meat, drinking alcohol and chasing after girls. But Mohan thought it was a wonderful idea.

'I will never touch meat or wine,' he promised. He was longing to go. Finally, his mother gave in. And Mohan left Kasturba and his year-old son, Harilal, to set off on his London adventure.

He was not even twenty years old.

He first went to the port-city of Bombay (now called Mumbai), from where ships sailed to Europe. The people from his caste were not happy at all. The community leaders in Bombay got together and took him to task.

'You will break all the rules of our religion,' they said. 'No one can go to Europe and stay pure.'

'I have promised my mother that I will not drink alcohol or eat meat, and I never break promises,' argued Mohan.

'We will treat you as an outcaste,' they threatened. But Mohan was unmoved.

And finally, on 4 September 1888, he set sail for London.

But poor Mohan wasn't prepared at all. His troubles started on the voyage itself. He had no idea how to eat using a knife and fork. He was embarrassed. He began to have his meals in his cabin, by himself, where no one could see him and he could eat with his fingers, the way he did at home.

Learning a New Way of Life

Landing in London was just as hard. Mohan had saved his one and only white flannel suit for the day he would touch English shores, thinking it would be perfect. To his further embarrassment, though, people didn't wear white flannel in the beginning of the London winter. He felt he was the only one in the whole of England wearing white.

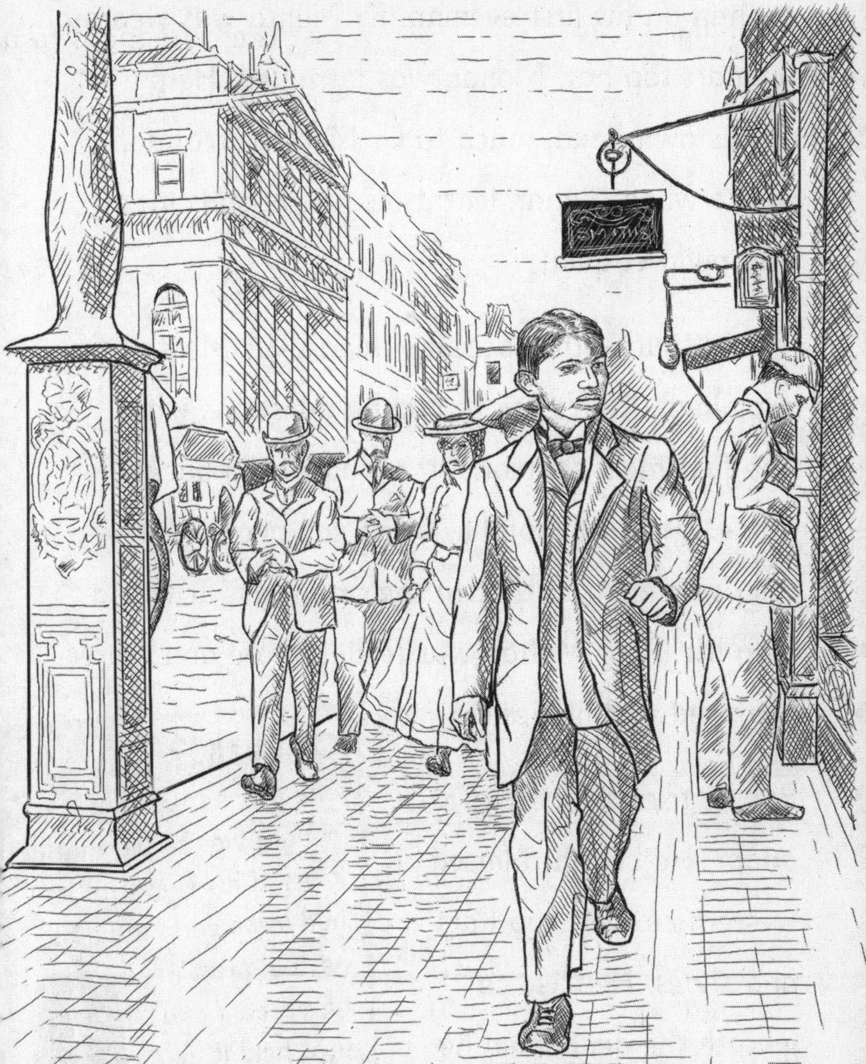

A family friend, called Dr Mehta, came to meet Mohan on his first evening. Dr Mehta was wearing a smart top hat. Mohan was intrigued. He put it on his own head, much to Dr Mehta's irritation. That's when Mohan learnt his first lessons in European etiquette.

'Never touch other people's things,' Dr Mehta explained. 'Don't ask too many questions when you first meet someone, the way we do back home. Don't talk loudly. Don't call people "sir"— only servants say that to their masters.' It was a long list. Poor Mohan was feeling more and more confused and homesick.

But he tried his best to adapt. He bought himself western clothes, top hats and shoes. He tried to imitate the gentlemen he saw around him. But what really bothered him was the food.

Oh Really?
The first hat Gandhi bought was so big that it covered his eyes. But he had large ears, so luckily, he could rest it on his ears and they held it up, off his eyes.

Starved for Food

'Ugh! I can't bear these boiled vegetables with no spices,' Mohan said to himself disgustedly, looking at the tasteless mush that passed for vegetable stew. He would have a breakfast of oatmeal porridge, and then starve for the better part of the day. Or he would eat spinach with bread and jam. Every day, he thought longingly of the food his mother cooked.

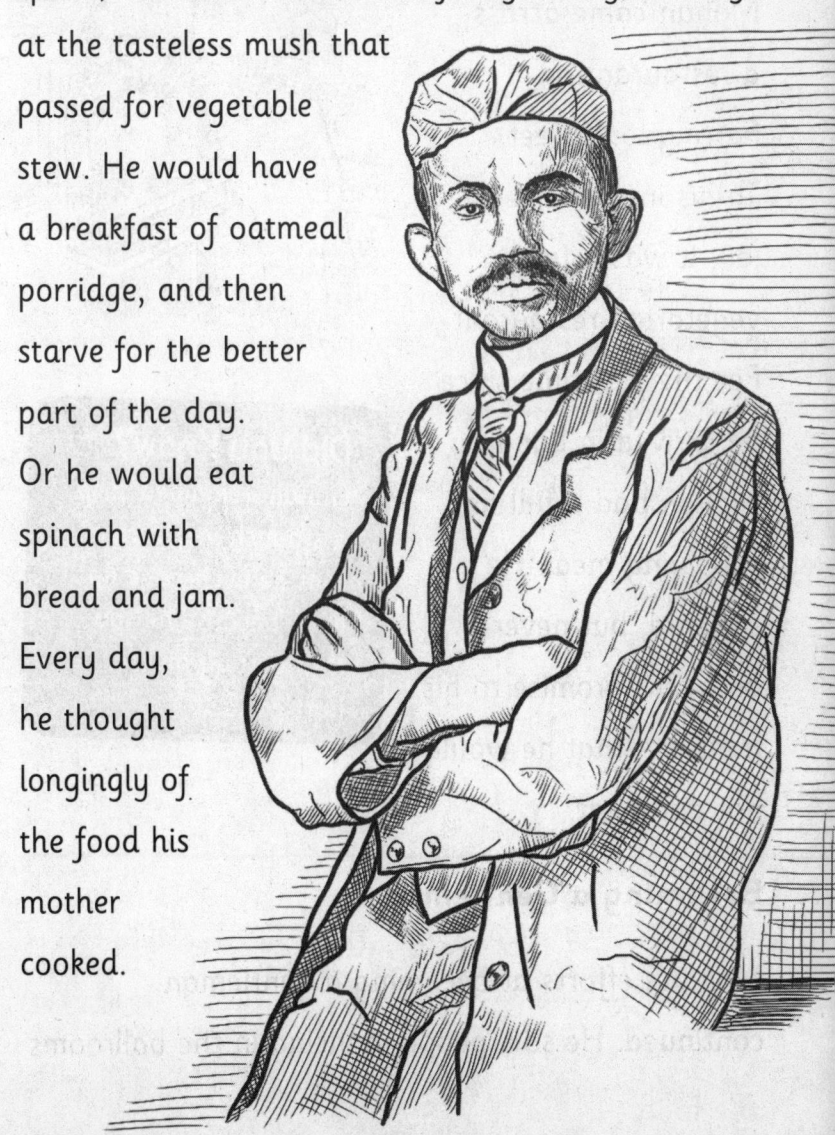

One day, when he was walking around and exploring London, Mohan came across a restaurant on Farringdon Street. To his immense joy, it was a fully vegetarian restaurant. For the first time since he arrived in London, Mohan had a full and satisfying meal. He suffered, but never broke his promise to his mother—that he would not eat meat.

Did You Know?
Gandhi remained such a staunch vegetarian that he even gave up milk, because he saw that getting milked hurt cows.

Becoming a Gentleman

Mohan's efforts at becoming a gentleman continued. He saw people dancing in the ballrooms

of London, so he joined
a ballroom-dancing class,
paying the princely sum
of three guineas (a lot
of money in those days)
for one term. He tried
to learn the violin.
He learnt how to knot
a tie and began to spend
hours in front of the mirror, perfecting his look.
He even spent as much as nineteen shillings for a
chimney-pot hat, which only made him look funny.
It depleted his meagre savings but he went ahead
and spent it anyway.

Now Mohan had begun
to look and walk like an
English gentleman.
But not quite talk like
one yet. So he set
another task for himself.
He had to learn to speak the Queen's English.

> **Oh Really?**
> Mohandas bought a violin for three pounds. He hired a violin teacher and practiced hard. But he just couldn't get the hang of it. Finally, he sold the violin when he decided it just wasn't worth all the time and effort.

> **Did You Know?**
> It is said that when Gandhi spoke English, he had a hint of an Irish accent. That's because one of his earliest English teachers was an Irishman.

'It will be important in law practice,' he told himself. Though he knew basic English, he decided that he should pass the London Matriculation exam. This meant a whole lot of extra work. Plus, he had to learn Latin in order to pass this exam. But Mohan was never afraid of hard work. He studied from morning till night, and in addition to his law degree, wrote his matriculation exam, though he didn't pass the dreaded Latin exam. That doesn't mean he gave up. He tried again. He learnt French too.

> ### It's True!
> Mohan realized he was spending too much money. He moved to a really tiny room, paying very little rent. He bought a stove and started cooking his own oatmeal breakfast. Dinner was bread and cocoa. Soon, he actually began to like the taste of boiled spinach, which he had hated when he'd first arrived.

Finally, in June 1891, Mohan became a proper lawyer. His studies in London were over and it was time to go home to India.

He couldn't wait to get back. He was longing to meet his beloved mother. Upon his arrival, his brother Laxmidas came to meet him at the docks. There was terrible news waiting for him. In his absence, his mother had died. It was a great shock—even worse than when he lost his father. Mohan was struck with grief. But in his usual way, he decided to move on.

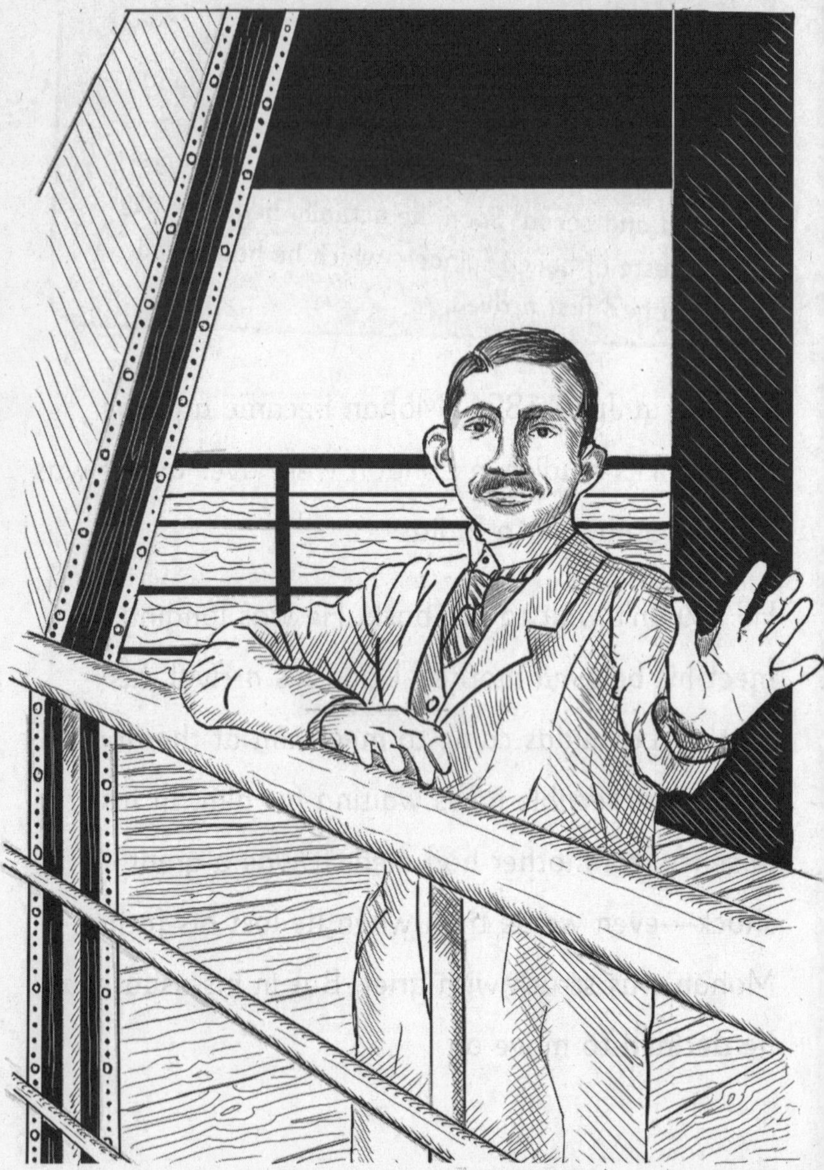

3 Off to Africa

Returning home posed new challenges. The people of Mohan's caste were still unhappy about how Mohan had gone to London in the teeth of their opposition. They were not willing to let him back into their caste.

> **It's True!**
> Because Mohan was thrown out of his caste, for a long time, he was not allowed to even drink water at his own sister's or brother's homes. But Mohan didn't protest. He went along with it, until he was finally reinstated in the caste.

Here was a new problem. Though Mohan had mastered British law, he had no idea of how things happened in India. India was so much more complex, with different castes, languages and issues.

How on earth could he practise in India?

The first time he took on his own case, Mohan was completely tongue-tied in court. He felt as if everyone in court was laughing at him.

> ### Did You Know?
> Once Gandhi went to a British officer he knew from his London days. His brother had sent him to ask for a favour. But the officer bluntly refused to help and had Gandhi thrown out of his office. Gandhi felt insulted. But he was advised to swallow the insult. 'The British rule us. That's just the way it is,' was the advice he got.

He was so ashamed that he decided to give up law and become a teacher instead.

Mohan spotted this advertisement in the papers one day. He promptly applied. To his dismay, he was turned down because he wasn't a graduate in India even though he had done his matriculation in London!

WANTED

AN ENGLISH TEACHER
to teach one hour daily

DAILY SALARY Rs 75

Mohan was crestfallen. Now what would he do?

He decided to set up shop in Rajkot. He did small jobs. During this period, he got to know his spirited wife, Kasturba, better. He tried to teach her the European way of life.

'Come, I will teach you how to eat with a knife and fork,' he'd say.

'Why, what's wrong with my hands? They work as well, if not better than your knife and fork,' she'd retort defiantly.

They squabbled and argued, but slowly grew to love and respect one another. They'd had one more son by now, whom they named Manilal.

But Mohan was not quite happy with his work. His brother had given up a lot to send him to London. But what was he doing? Small jobs in Rajkot? His plans of being a great barrister* were not coming true at all!

*A barrister is a lawyer who passes an exam and is allowed to practise in higher courts of law.

Opportunity Knocks

Then one day, opportunity came knocking on Mohan's door. His brother got a letter from a firm in Porbandar. Here's what the letter said:

We have business in South Africa. We have a big court case going on. If we win that case, we will get £40,000. Our lawyers there are not making much headway. Your brother has studied in London. If you send him there for one year, we will pay him £105.

Mohan jumped at the opportunity. After all, his business in Rajkot wasn't doing all that well. This was a chance to at least send back £105 to his brother. So once again, Mohan packed his bags and bid farewell to his young wife and sons, and in 1893, off he went on his second adventure—this time to South Africa.

A man called Abdulla Sheth came to receive Mohan when he landed at the Port of Durban in South Africa. After helping him settle down, Abdulla took Mohan to court. Mohan, silently observing things as always, noticed people were behaving rather snobbishly towards Abdullah, who didn't seem to mind. In fact, he noticed that all Indians were being looked at with a little bit of suspicion and a lot of disdain.

'Hmm,' thought Gandhi. 'Must investigate this.'

Tale of the Turban

He didn't have to wait long. He had worn a turban to court, as was his habit. After staring long and hard at him, the magistrate asked Gandhi to remove the turban. This infuriated Gandhi.

'I will not,' he said defiantly. 'Is there a law against wearing turbans in court?'

He argued fiercely. He wrote letters to newspapers. He spoke to groups of Indian people, telling them that authorities had no business telling him how to dress. He never stopped wearing his turban to court.

This was the beginning of a long battle between Gandhi and the authorities—and one that was to change the fate of India's history.

4 Fighting Injustice

From the very minute that Gandhi landed in South Africa, he felt as if someone was suffocating him. Do you know why? The Indians who lived in South Africa were being constantly insulted by the white Britishers who ruled there.

Because a lot of Indians had gone there to earn money as labourers or coolies, the white people called all Indians coolies. If you had brown skin, you were a 'coolie'. If you were an Indian lawyer, you were a 'coolie lawyer'. If you were an Indian doctor, you were a 'coolie doctor'.

One day, things came to a head. Gandhi was travelling to Pretoria by train. His clients had given him a first-class ticket. Gandhi was sitting comfortably in the first-class coach, when the ticket inspector came.

'You cannot sit here,' he said rudely to Gandhi.

'Why? I have a first-class ticket,' retorted Gandhi.

'Because those are the rules,' said the ticket inspector. Gandhi refused to budge.

'Well, then, I shall have to remove you by force,' the inspector said. He called a few people and had Gandhi and his luggage thrown off the train.

Gandhi sat on the platform all night. He sat still, but his mind was working fast.

Something Snaps

Something snapped in his mind. This was intolerable.

'People who accept injustice are just as guilty as people who impose it,' he thought. He decided that he could not sit back and let this continue.

His arrival in Pretoria was just as difficult. He had nowhere to stay and no hotel would accommodate him because of his brown skin. Finally, an African man, who was standing nearby and watching Gandhi, came to his rescue.

'I will take you to an American hotel. Americans don't bother about such things.' He took Gandhi to Johnston's Family Hotel. Mr Johnston was a decent man.

'I will give you a room to stay. But I am sorry, I cannot allow you to have dinner in the main dining room,' he said apologetically. 'You see, all my other guests will be offended.' So Gandhi stayed in the hotel only for a night, but ate alone. He was getting used to this kind of treatment.

> **Did You Know?**
> No hotel would give Gandhi a room to stay during his time in Pretoria. Finally, he convinced a poor woman, the wife of a baker, to rent him a small room for thirty-five shillings a week.

During his stay in Pretoria, Gandhi went for long walks. His route took him past the house of President Kruger, who was the leader at that time. One day, there was a new guard at the head of the road.

Seeing Gandhi's brown skin, he came and stood in Gandhi's way.

'You cannot walk on this road,' the guard said rudely, pushing Gandhi.

'Why? Isn't this a public road?' Gandhi asked, trying to control his anger.

'No, it is not for people like you.' Saying this, the guard shoved Gandhi to the ground and kicked him hard. Gandhi saw red. He wanted to hit back, but his discipline and love of peace stopped him. Besides, the guard was following the rules. It was not his fault.

'The solution is not to stop this man. The solution is to change the rules. We must strike at the root of the problem,' he thought. He got up, dusted his clothes and walked away.

Gathering a Force

Gandhi began to act. And when Gandhi acted, he wasted no time. First, he studied what the law in South Africa said. To his horror, the law was not only unfair, it was downright cruel to Indians.

- Indians could not walk on public footpaths.
- They could not go outdoors after 9 p.m. without a permit.
- They could only travel third class.
- They could not stay in most hotels.
- They could not enter many cafeterias and restaurants.
- They could not own property.
- They could not vote.

This was too much for Gandhi. He got together a group of Indians who had been suffering this treatment silently. Among them were Hindus, Muslims, Sikhs and Parsis—all of whom had been subjected to this kind of prejudice.

'We cannot stand for this treatment,' Gandhi thundered. He was surprised at himself. How did such a shy man find the courage to speak to so many people in such a public place? It was his anger at the injustice that gave him strength.

5 Soldiers of Truth

The year was 1894. Gandhi had successfully resolved the case for which he had come to South Africa. He could have returned to India. But he just could not bear to turn his back on the Indian people in South Africa.

'I have been sent here with a larger purpose,' he thought. Instead of going back, he worked harder than ever. He started an organization called the Natal Indian Congress. He worked day and night, helping sort out the affairs of Indians in trouble. Soon he became famous. The British authorities hated him. But the Indian and black communities loved him. Everyone wanted him to stay on.

> ### Did You Know?
> South African law treated black and 'coloured' people as inferior; there were harsh rules and punishments were meted out to them if they did not obey. But white people were exempt from these rules. This was known as apartheid.

'Kasturba has been bringing up our sons by herself. It is time we were together,' he thought. He decided to bring his family to South Africa. Off he went on the long voyage, and returned with Kasturba and their two little sons.

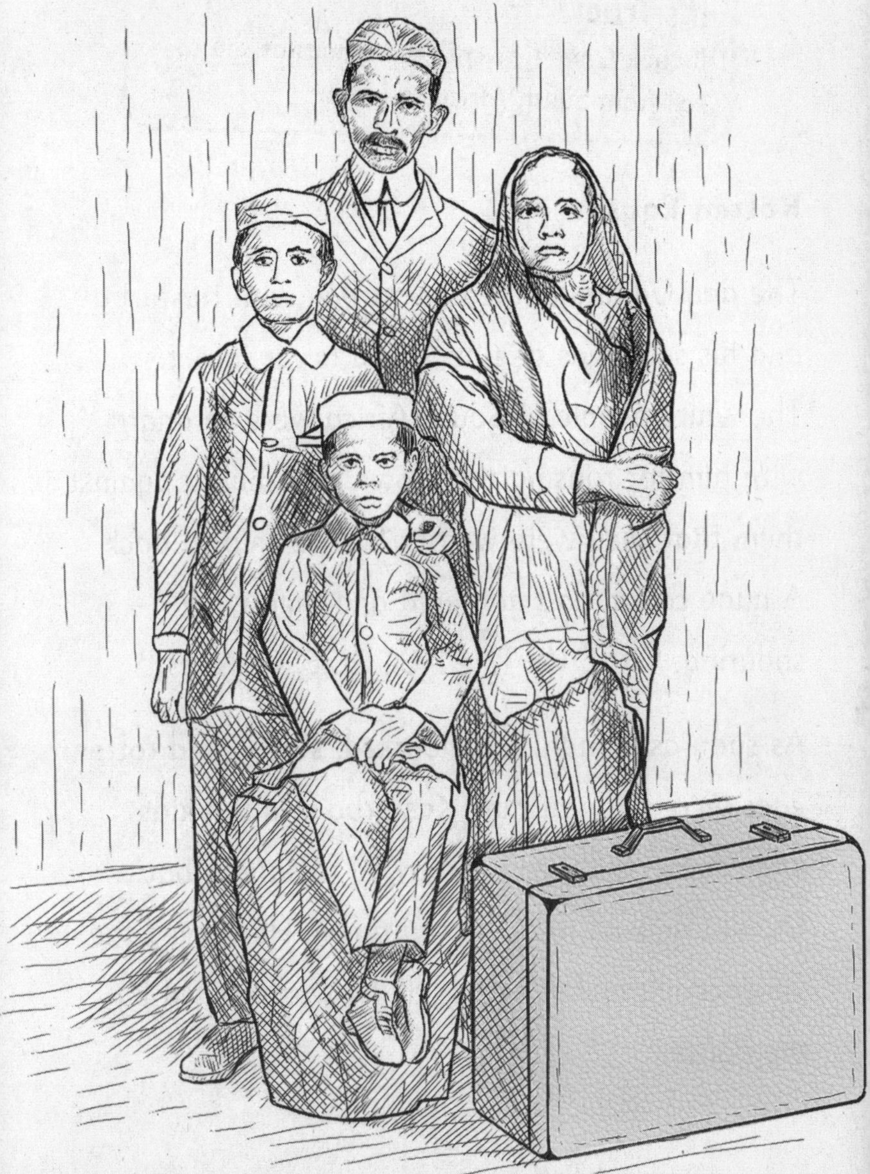

> **It's True!**
> It took Gandhi twenty-three days at sea to sail from South Africa to India.

Rotten Eggs

The day Gandhi landed in Durban with Kasturba and his sons was one he would never forget. The white people of South Africa were so angry with him for rousing the brown community against them that they were waiting for his ship to dock. A huge crowd had gathered and they were shouting, 'GIVE US THAT COOLIE, GANDHI!'

As soon as Gandhi disembarked, stones and rotten eggs were flung at him. Kasturba and the kids were successfully whisked away to safety, but Gandhi refused to be cowed down. He braved the violence without reacting, till he was rescued by the police.

Did You Know?
Gandhi disguised himself as an Indian constable to escape the crowd. That is how he got away from the mob that was baying for his blood.

Trying to Get on the Right Side of the British

In 1899, the British went to war with the Dutch Boers. The Boers were people of Dutch descent living in this region. Their fight against the British for independence was called the Boer War. Now Gandhi saw a chance to impress the British, in the hope that this would get them to change their attitude towards Indians. He collected large groups of Indians, who helped nurse wounded British soldiers. But it made no difference.

In fact, during his stay in
Africa, Gandhi did lots of
things to try and build
the confidence of the
Indians there. He even
started three football
clubs so that Indians
could play a sport. They
all had the same name—Passive Resisters
Soccer Club.

> **Oh Really?**
> Gandhi and his corps would carry wounded soldiers for twenty-five miles at a time, from the war zone to the hospitals, so that they could be treated.

The Force of Truth

Now Gandhi hit upon a new way to try and change
the unfair laws. He called it satyagraha: *satya*
(truth) and *agraha* (force). He decided the best way
was a peaceful but stubborn insistence on truth.
He organized protests and rallies, but no one was
allowed to raise a hand. He was even sent to jail,
but he was such a model and peaceful prisoner that
he had to be released.

By now, Gandhi had thousands of followers. They called themselves satyagrahis. Gandhi started settlements in which many satyagrahis lived a simple life. A wealthy German-South African man called Hermann Kallenbach was so impressed with Gandhi that he gave him 1100 acres of land, on which Gandhi set up the community. He named it Tolstoy Farm. Everyone worked hard on the farm.

> **Did You Know?**
> Hermann Kallenbach remained close friends with Gandhi all his life. In fact, Gandhi called him his 'white brother'.

> **It's True!**
> Gandhi couldn't afford a washerman to wash and iron his clothes. So he and Kasturba learnt how to wash their own clothes. Once, he put too much starch in his collar, making it so stiff that he couldn't even turn his head around. Everyone laughed at him. But ridicule never bothered Gandhi. He simply didn't care.

How Dare You?

Despite his groundbreaking work towards helping Indians in South Africa, Gandhi was yet to learn an important lesson about taking people for granted.

Like the other satyagrahis, the Gandhis too lived a very simple life. They cooked their own food and wore simple clothes. But what bothered Kasturba was toilet duty.

The camps had no bathrooms and so people had to use chamber pots, which they had to clean themselves.

Kasturba hated doing this, but she had got used to her fiery husband's habits, so she did her work without question. She went about the job sulkily. But one day, he asked her to clean someone else's chamber pot. That was the last straw. She refused.

'How dare you refuse?'

Gandhi roared at her. 'Do you think you are above all this?'

This time Kasturba didn't hold back. She shouted right back at him, 'Just because I am your wife and I have nowhere to go, don't think I will put up with this.' She burst into tears and ran into the house.

Gandhi felt truly ashamed. In all his zeal, he had quite forgotten how much Kasturba had sacrificed for him.

Did You Know?

The barbers in South Africa refused to cut Gandhi's hair. So he decided to do it himself. Sitting awkwardly in front of a mirror, he snipped and chopped. Naturally, it was not neat at all. When his friends saw him the next day, they all laughed at him. 'Looks like a rat got at your hair,' they sniggered. Did it bother Gandhi? Not a bit!

The Final Reward

All the fights, protests and silent marches finally had an impact. In July 1914, the South African government at long last passed the Indian Relief Act. Many of the unfair laws and taxes imposed on Indians were lifted. It was a great victory.

Gandhi's work in South Africa was done. His original assignment had been for just one year. But he had stayed for more than twenty.

In these twenty years, he had become a famous and confident lawyer, whose greatest passion was to fight against injustice.

By now, Gandhi and Kasturba were the parents of four young boys. Along with his brood, he set sail for India. His country needed him.

Did You Know?
When they were leaving, people gave Kasturba and Gandhi lots of gifts, including a gold watch and a very expensive diamond necklace. Gandhi donated them to the local Congress office, who would use it for the people.

6 Coming Home to India

While Gandhi had been busy solving the problems of Indians in South Africa, things had reached a boiling point in India. The year was 1914. People across India were angry and fed up with the British and tried every way to get rid of them.

They had heard a lot about Gandhi's work in South Africa. He was welcomed home almost like a messiah, someone who would help solve their problems.

In his usual way, Gandhi first wanted to understand what was happening.

'I want to see how the people of my country are living,' he said. He took off on a train journey across the length and breadth of the vast nation. He saw the way people lived. He saw the anger that was simmering. He was depressed at the unhygienic conditions.

53

The Indian leaders had formed an organization called the Indian National Congress. There were freedom fighters like Pherozeshah Mehta, Dadabhai Naoroji, Gopal Krishna Gokhale, Sardar Vallabhbhai Patel and Jawaharlal Nehru, who were all part of the Congress. They approached Gandhi to help them in the fight for independence.

The Peaceful Camp

'I would like to start an ashram—a settlement like I had in South Africa,' Gandhi told them. 'I have my volunteers. I will be able to help in the freedom struggle from there.'

He set up an ashram called Satyagraha Ashram in Ahmedabad, in his home state of Gujarat, right on the banks of River Sabarmati. He and his band of followers lived there together. They led a simple life. They wove their own cloth, grew their own fruit and vegetables. They had very few possessions.

Gandhi believed that the first step in helping people fight for independence was to make them self-reliant. By spinning his own yarn and having almost no material needs, he was demonstrating to them how they could truly be their own masters.

Harijans: People of God

Yet another of his great beliefs was that all people are equal. India was riddled with the ills of the caste system at that time. This system kept out from normal life a big group of people whom they called the 'untouchables'.

> ## The Caste System in India
> The Hindu caste system divided all people into four groups. At the top were the Brahmins (the religious caste); next came the Kshatriyas (the warrior caste); then came the Vaishyas (the merchants and traders); finally the Shudras (the servant class).
> The Brahmins were the most respected, while the Shudras were the least. The untouchables were outside the system altogether. These people were considered impure, and they were made to do all the dirtiest work. According to the system, you were born into a caste and couldn't change it—ever.

But Gandhi believed all men and women are the same in the eyes of God. He called the so-called untouchables Harijans (meaning people of God).

One day, a homeless Harijan couple with a little baby came looking for shelter in the ashram. The people living there were aghast. Though they followed Gandhi, they could simply not accept being close to a Harijan—leave alone living side by side and eating meals together. So deep was their prejudice.

But Gandhi welcomed them with open arms.

'If you cannot accept them, you cannot accept me,' he said. Gandhi was clear. 'If you are unhappy with them sharing your room and your food, you are free to leave the ashram. But they will stay.' And they did. Even Kasturba, who sulked for some time, overcame her sulks and grew to respect and accept this way of thinking.

From Gandhiji to Bapu

Gandhi spent a lot of time with people. He wanted to get rid of ignorance. He opened schools and taught people the importance of hygiene. People started coming to him for advice. They loved him and started calling him Bapu.

Did You Know?
Rabindranath Tagore, the great philosopher and poet, was so moved by Gandhi's beliefs that he gave him the title Mahatma. All over the world, Gandhi is now known as Mahatma Gandhi.

7 We Will Not Cooperate

Gandhi could not bear injustice. Once, he saw how some factory owners in Ahmedabad were exploiting their labourers. He organized a strike and helped the labourers get their due.

Slowly but surely, Gandhi's methods of satyagraha and peaceful protest were gaining popularity. He used satyagraha to help farmers from being unfairly squeezed for money and taxes by the landlords in a place called Champaran, in Bihar. He organized peaceful rallies. When the British saw how strong this tiny man was becoming, they arrested him. To their shock and horror, thousands and thousands of people gathered and protested against Gandhi's arrest. They were forced to release him.

Oh Really?

Gandhi usually cooked for himself. One day, he got a severe tummy upset. Kasturba made him some porridge of grain and milk to soothe his stomach. But Gandhi had given up milk. He was adamant about not having any. It was only when his doctors pointed out that he could not help in the freedom struggle if he did not recover that he agreed to have milk. But he still refused cow's milk, because the methods of milking cows were cruel. Very reluctantly, he agreed to have goat's milk.

A Disaster in the Making

One morning, Gandhi was reading the paper, sitting on the porch of his hut in the ashram. His eyes grew wide. He was reading about a law that the British were planning to pass. This was called the Rowlatt Act. Under this law, it was suggested that people could be arrested and jailed without the benefit of a fair trial in court.

'If this happens, protestors will be jailed without cause,' thought Gandhi. 'We must stop this from being turned into a law.'

He called for a full day of non-cooperation. The message spread across India like wildfire. It was supposed to be a day of hartal or strike. One morning, the British people woke up to find that no one in the entire country had come to work. Factories, shops, offices—everything was silent and shut.

The hartal would have been a success, but sadly, in some places there were outbursts of violence.

'Violence in any form is unacceptable,' said Gandhi. He stopped the hartal. The hateful Rowlatt Act was passed.

A Terrible Massacre

The people of the country were even more angry now. It was getting difficult to control their protests. One incident acted like a match to firewood, sparking explosive violence.

It was Baisakhi. More than 10,000 people assembled peacefully to celebrate the festival in a walled public garden called Jallianwala Bagh in the city of Amritsar, in Punjab. Perhaps they did not know that the British had banned large gatherings. The group was non-violent. But an official called General Dyer was infuriated at the turnout. He ordered his troops to open fire. There was nowhere to run, for Dyer had ordered all gates to be closed. His troops kept firing for ten minutes. Thousands of people were killed and injured.

63

> **Did You Know?**
> General Dyer is called the Butcher of Amritsar because of this horrific act.

Boycott

Now there was no stopping the violence. Gandhi was shattered. His whole belief system rested on non-violence, but he was unable to control his own countrymen. He decided to become even more active but do things his way—through non-cooperation.

The main objective of the British in India had been to increase their wealth through trade. One way of doing this was by controlling the buying and selling of cloth in India. Cotton grown in India was sent to England, made into cloth there and then sold in India.

Gandhi decided to boycott anything made in England and persuaded people to only buy swadeshi goods. This was called the Swadeshi movement. It slowed down the British economy in India and made the struggle for independence even stronger.

> **Did You Know?**
> Swadeshi means 'of your own country'.

The Khadi Movement

'Let us only wear homespun khadi,' Gandhi told people. He would spin the coarse cotton material every day and taught his followers to do the same. Slowly, thousands of Indians switched to homespun khadi, crippling British cloth factories. His spinning wheel became a symbol of India's struggle for independence.

Meanwhile, Gandhi would walk miles every day, talking to people in the smallest villages, gathering their support for the independence movement. He continued to organize strikes and protests. He was arrested several times, but every time, the authorities had to let him go because of pressure from the public.

A Pinch of Salt

The British had taken control of the salt that was made in India. People were not allowed to make their own salt, even though it was easy to do so. They were forced to buy expensive salt from the

British, and pay tax on it. This was yet another unfair practice that made Gandhi angry.

'Salt is a necessity. How can poor people pay so much for salt?' he argued. In his usual way, he resolved to do something about it. He decided to march to the seashore and make his own salt as a mark of protest.

Marching for Justice

And so began a long, long walk. On 12 March 1930, Gandhi and seventy-two of his followers started their walk. They had to cover more than 400 kilometres across the state of Gujarat to reach the sea at the village of Dandi.
As they walked, more and more people joined them, including Jawaharlal Nehru and Sardar Vallabhbhai Patel.

You would think that this would be an impossible feat for a thin, frail man like Gandhi. The British certainly thought so, which is why they made no effort to stop him. They thought he would collapse long before he reached his journey's end. But what they didn't know was that Gandhi was a tireless walker.

> ### That's Amazing!
> It is said that Gandhi used to walk eighteen kilometres a day. Which means he could well have walked around the earth twice over during his lifetime. So to him, the walk to Dandi was child's play.

Gandhi and his followers marched on. Along the way, people gave them food and water. There were Hindus, Muslims, Christians and Sikhs; there were men, women, children and aged people. They walked tirelessly through rain and sun.

After twenty-five days of walking, Gandhi and his followers reached the sea at Dandi, a seaside village. Defying the law, Gandhi went forward and picked up a handful of salt from the shore.

British troops were waiting to stop them. They hit people with sticks, but no one retaliated. The injured were carried away and other protestors took their place.

Gandhi, Nehru and Patel were all arrested, along with thousands of others.

The World Watches

It was an event that was watched by the whole world. The British could no longer ignore what the Indians were trying to tell them: 'Go home to your own country, and leave us alone.'

Did You Know?
The mixture of salt and sand that Gandhi scooped up was sold many years later at an auction.

8 The Final Fight

Gandhi had become world-famous. The British got messages from across the globe, demanding that Gandhi be released. They realized that the only way they could salvage the situation was to get Gandhi on their side.

They invited him to London in September 1931 to discuss what was to be done. Gandhi went cheerfully, very hopeful that he would convince the British to leave India. There were discussions at a meeting called the Round Table Conference. But no conclusion was reached and Gandhi went back disappointed.

Did You Know?
In London, Gandhi refused to wear western clothes like he had when he was young. He even had tea with King George V and Queen Mary wearing only his dhoti with a shawl.

Oh Really?
Winston Churchill, who went on to become prime minister of United Kingdom, scornfully referred to Gandhi as the 'half-naked fakir'. Little did he know he would be forced to bow down to this tiny man.

Back in Jail

As soon as he got back to India, Gandhi started another protest. He was promptly put in jail. Kasturba, who had been following her husband's example, was already in jail. The British had kept a separate court for the untouchables, following the Indian caste system. This upset Gandhi. Even though he was in jail, he began to fast, demanding that untouchables be treated equally. This time, he decided he would fast until he died if he had to, unless the British changed the system. Worried that he would die and that might spark riots, they agreed to his demands and released him.

As soon as he was released, Gandhi was back in action.

Quit India or Else . . .

In 1942, he started a new movement. 'QUIT INDIA!' an entire nation roared. Gandhi wanted there to be silent protests. But people had lost patience. There were several outbreaks of violence. This saddened Gandhi.

World War II had broken out in 1939. The British volunteered Indian troops. But unlike the Boer War, this time, Gandhi did not cooperate.

Did You Know?

Gandhi was so disturbed by Hitler, who was ordering the killing of Jews by the thousands, that he wrote a letter to Hitler in 1940. Here is an excerpt:

Dear friend,
... You are the one person in the world who can prevent a war which may reduce humanity to the savage state ...
... Will you listen to the appeal of one who has deliberately shunned the method of war, not without considerable success?
... Any way, I anticipate your forgiveness, if I have erred in writing to you.
I remain
Your sincere friend
M.K. Gandhi

'Why should we fight for other countries' freedom when we don't have our own?' was his logic. There were riots and violence all over India as people continued to protest against the British. Once again, British authorities held Gandhi responsible and arrested him.

A Partnership Ends

Kasturba, who had been Gandhi's faithful companion for so many years, was seriously ill. He tended to her lovingly, never leaving her side in her last days. One February day in 1944, she passed away. He held her in her last moments. He himself was weak and tired.

Freedom Is Near

In May 1945, World War II ended. The British had lost a lot during the war—people, money and resources. They no longer had the will or the energy to manage India. They decided to give India its freedom.

A New Problem to Tackle

But now there was a new issue. Muslims and Hindus were not getting along. There were riots amongst them. Indian political leaders had discussions with the British, and it was decided that India would be split into two independent countries—India and Pakistan. Pakistan would be dominated by Muslims, and India, by Hindus. Nehru would be prime minister of India and Muhammad Ali Jinnah would be leader of Pakistan. Not just that, Pakistan itself would have two parts: West Pakistan, to the west of India, and East Pakistan, to the east of Bengal. In fact, an outcome of this historic event called Partition was that it was Bengal that was divided into

East Pakistan and West Bengal. It tore apart families, and people had to leave behind their entire lives when they moved across the new borders.

Independence At Last

Finally, at midnight on 15 August 1947, India became free. One day earlier, Pakistan was born as a nation too. All of India celebrated.
But Gandhi, all alone on a wooden cot in Calcutta (now Kolkata), was sad.

'I have failed,' he said. 'The British may have gone, but Hindus and Muslims have been divided.' It had been his life's mission to bring people together.

Gandhi was now almost eighty years old. His life had been full of struggle, jail, fasts and hard work. While he was weak in the body, he was still strong in the mind.

End of an Era

There was a small group of staunch Hindu people who felt Gandhi had betrayed Hindus by allowing a Muslim nation to be formed. They also felt anger at many of Gandhi's peaceful policies.

On 30 January 1948, Gandhi was leaving for a prayer meeting in Delhi. He was walking, leaning on two supporters on either side, when suddenly he fell to the ground. He had been shot by a man called Nathuram Godse, who was one of the Hindu extremists who did not like Gandhi's methods.

'Hey, Ram' were Gandhi's last words.

There was national mourning, as an entire country was cast into gloom. Their beloved father was no more.

He had won India her independence, but given his life in the process.

Thousands of people thronged the streets. There were riots. All of India was devastated.

> **Did You Know?**
> Gandhi's funeral procession was eight kilometres long.

In fact, the whole world mourned. A little man in a dhoti had taught the world a lesson they would never forget—that anything could be achieved through peace.

9 Gandhi Factopedia

Mahatma Gandhi was a tiny man with very big ideas. He also had a sense of humour, and he made a lot of jokes about himself too. There are many little things about the man and his life that are interesting to know about. Here's a snapshot:

Friday's Child: Gandhi was born on a Friday, India became independent on a Friday and he died on a Friday.

Gandhi didn't use soap to bathe. Instead he used a piece of stone given to him by Mirabehn, a devout follower.

Gandhi didn't own anything that was costly or valuable. But once someone gave him a fountain pen that was quite expensive. It was stolen. Gandhi swore to never again own anything that would tempt anyone.

By sharpening a wooden holder, Gandhi made his own pen. This was called a *kitta*. The first letter he wrote using this kitta was to Lord Mountbatten, who was the viceroy of India.

Gandhi lost all his teeth as he grew old, but he hated wearing dentures. He would carry them in the folds of his dhoti, and slip them on only while eating.

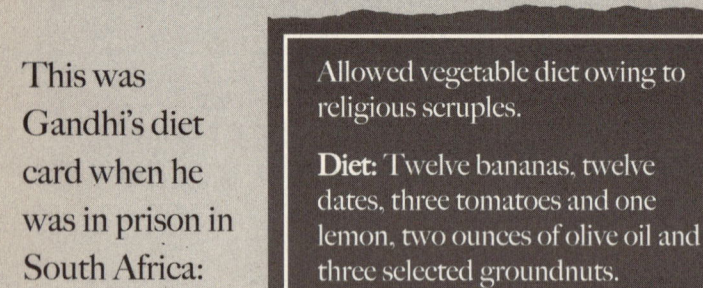

This was Gandhi's diet card when he was in prison in South Africa:

> Allowed vegetable diet owing to religious scruples.
>
> **Diet:** Twelve bananas, twelve dates, three tomatoes and one lemon, two ounces of olive oil and three selected groundnuts.

While in South Africa, Gandhi started a newspaper called Indian Opinion. He used this to make people aware of the plight of Indians in South Africa.

The only belonging that Gandhi cherished till the day he died was his watch. He felt even a single minute of the day should not be wasted and was punctual to a fault.

When Gandhi took off for the Dandi march, the viceroy did not order that he be stopped. Because he was sure that Gandhi's blood pressure would rise so much that he would not survive the walk.

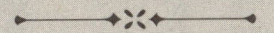

Once a reporter asked Gandhi, 'Why do you always travel third class in a train?'

'Because there is no fourth class,' came the prompt reply.

Gandhi travelled a lot—by train, by bus or on foot. But he always found time to write a quick postcard to his friends and followers. He found postcards the most useful—economical and handy.

Once, during his visits to rural India, Gandhi woke up to the sound of music and drumbeats. A bunch of villagers came up to his hut. They presented him with fruits and flowers. 'You are God,' they said. 'As soon as you stepped into the village, it rained.'

'Are you crazy?' Gandhi objected. He immediately explained away this ridiculous notion. He did not believe in superstition because he felt it made people blind and unreasonable.

The famous Charlie Chaplin greatly admired Gandhi. Once, when Gandhi was in London, Chaplin wrote him a letter requesting a meeting.

'Who is this Charlie Chaplin?' Gandhi asked his followers. He was not impressed by Chaplin's fame as an actor. But when he heard that he supported Gandhi's beliefs, he agreed to meet him.

One of Gandhi's great hopes was to eliminate poverty. He disdained machines that made people lose jobs. One day someone asked him, 'Are you against all machines?'

'I am not,' he replied. 'The body is an amazing machine. I am against the craze for labour-saving machinery that puts thousands of people out of jobs and on the streets.'

When Gandhi was about to meet King George for tea in London, dressed in his simple dhoti, a news reporter asked, 'Mr Gandhi, are you properly dressed to meet the king of England?'

'My dear man, the king is wearing enough clothes for both of us,' Gandhi replied cheerfully.

People from all over the world visited Gandhi. Once, a group of people from China came to meet him. They brought him a small gift—a statuette of three monkeys. When they explained what those monkeys symbolized—'see no evil, hear no evil and speak no evil'—Gandhi loved them so much that he kept the gift to remind him of these three important messages.

When Gandhi went to London for the Round Table Conference, instead of staying in luxurious hotels that were provided for him, he chose to stay in a place called Kingsley Hall, which was in the poorer part of London. He wished to stay near the less privileged and share their lives with them.

Gandhi loved cricket. He was a pretty good bowler and batsman too. Once when he was in London, he was invited to play in a friendly match organized by the Marylebone Cricket Club (MCC). He scored twenty-seven runs and took a wicket as well. His team won the match. He signed on the bat as the seventeenth player. That bat is still a treasured possession of the MCC in London.

There are more than fifty main roads named after Gandhi in India. And close to fifty more in other countries.

MAHATMA GANDHI ROAD

Time magazine is one of the world's foremost news magazines and is highly respected. In 1930, Gandhi was the first Indian to appear on the cover of the magazine as Man of the Year. There was an even bigger title he was runner-up for— *Time* magazine's Person of the Century. Finally, Albert Einstein won that title.

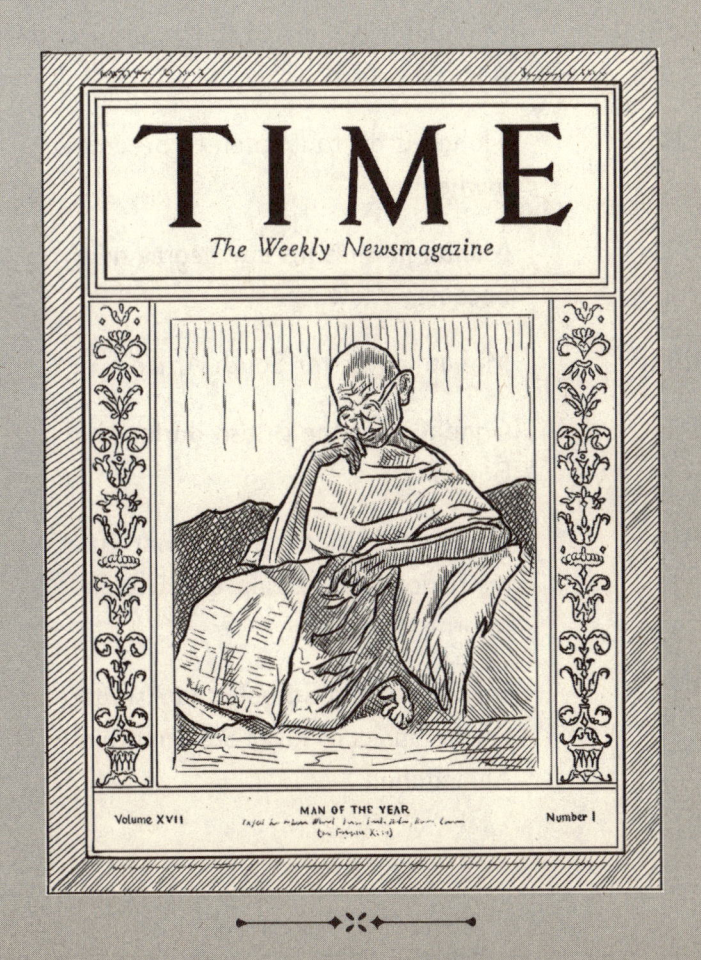

10 Timeline

2 October 1869: Mohandas Karamchand Gandhi is born.

1883: Mohandas is married to Kasturba at the age of thirteen.

1888: Mohan is off to London to become a lawyer.

1891: Mohan finishes his law degree and becomes a lawyer.

1893: Mohan leaves for South Africa.

1899: Gandhi helps the British during the Boer War.

1914: The South African government lifts the restrictions on Indians, and Gandhi returns to India.

1917: Gandhi sets up Satyagraha Ashram on the banks of River Sabarmati in Ahmedabad.

1917:	Gandhi's first effective satyagraha protest is held in Champaran.
1919:	The Jallianwala Bagh massacre takes place.
1930:	Gandhi launches the Swadeshi movement.
1930:	Gandhi marches to Dandi to pick up salt to defy the British law.
1931:	Gandhi goes to London for the Round Table Conference to find a solution.
1944:	Kasturba breathes her last.
1945:	World War II comes to an end.
1947:	India gets her independence.
30 January 1948:	Gandhi is shot dead by Nathuram Godse.

11 Bibliography

Dave, Jugatram. *Gandhiji*. Ahmedabad: Navajivan Trust, 2012.

Gandhi, M.K. *The Story of My Life*. Ahmedabad: Navajivan Trust, 2000.

Meghani, Mahendra, ed. and Jyoti Verma, trans. *Gandhi-Ganga*. Mumbai: Bombay Sarvodaya Mandal/Gandhi Book Center, 1968.

Roy, Rita, ed. *Everyone's Gandhi: A Collection of Gandhi Columns*. New Delhi: Gandhi Peace Foundation and Press Trust of India, 1997.

Zaidi, Begum Qudsia. *Our Bapu*. Ahmedabad: Navajivan Trust, 2010.

'A Place to Learn about Gandhi, His Life, Work & Philosophy', http://www.mkgandhi.org/.

'Mahatma Gandhi (1869–1948)', *The Divine Life Society*, http://www.dlshq.org/saints/gandhi.htm#england.

'Gandhi Back in India (1914–1948)', *Mani Bhavan Gandhi Sangrahalaya*, http://www.gandhi-manibhavan.org/aboutgandhi/biography_inindia.htm.